ANGEL SWANIGAN

The Fruit of My Thoughts

The Mental Blueprint for a Purpose Driven Life

First published by Conscious Publishing 2026

Copyright © 2026 by Angel Swanigan

All rights reserved. No part of this publication may be reproduced, stored or transmitted in any form or by any means, electronic, mechanical, photocopying, recording, scanning, or otherwise without written permission from the publisher. It is illegal to copy this book, post it to a website, or distribute it by any other means without permission.

Angel Swanigan asserts the moral right to be identified as the author of this work.

First edition

ISBN: 979-8-218-84139-3

This book was professionally typeset on Reedsy. Find out more at reedsy.com

Contents

Preface		iv
1	Chapter 1: Realizing That You Exist	1
2	Chapter 2: Hurting From Reverting	16
3	Chapter 3: Harvest Season	34
4	Chapter 4: Living in Full Bloom	43
Acknowledgments		60
About the Author		61

Preface

Reader Note: This book contains personal reflections and experiences related to trauma, emotional healing, sexual health, and mental well-being. Some chapters explore sensitive life events as part of a journey toward self-awareness and growth. Readers are encouraged to move through the material at their own pace and honor their emotional boundaries.

There comes a time in every life when silence starts speaking louder than words. For me, that silence came in the moments I stopped pretending to be okay. It came when I was forced to face the thoughts I'd been running from. This book was born from that stillness. The Fruit of My Thoughts isn't just a title, it's a truth. Every thought I've planted, every emotion I've faced, and every lesson I've harvested has shaped who I am today. What you're about to read isn't a manual or lecture. It's a mirror... a reflection of what happens when you stop surviving and start becoming.

For a long time, I didn't realize I even existed beyond what the world expected from me. I was alive, but not present. The awakening became Chapter one: Realizing That You Exist. It's where the journey begins; the first breath of self-awareness. But awareness isn't always peaceful. Growth exposes the parts of you you've avoided. The setbacks, the regressions, the moments when you slip back into who you used to be is discussed in Chapter Two: Hurting from Reverting. It's about the pain of recognizing progress and relapse as part of the same path.

Then something shifts, after all the tending, watering, and waiting, you start to see the results; not because life became easier, but because you became stronger. That's Chapter three: Harvest Season, the moment when what once felt like a struggle turns into wisdom, peace and purpose.

Finally Chapter four: Living in Full Bloom- where you learn to live freely, intentionally, and unapologetically, It's the chapter that reminds you that healing isn't about perfection, it's about integration. It's about letting your growth become the way you live. This book isn't about telling you how to live your life. It's about showing you what's possible when you start listening to your own thoughts and choosing the ones that serve your peace. Every page is a seed. Every story, a season and every season leads to fruit...the kind that nourishes not just your mind, but your soul.

This book is the fruit of my thoughts because I thought about writing it and it became physical. It is also the fruit of yours because you had an interest in this discussion and this book was brought to your attention. As you read, keep a journal next to you as there will be self-help exercises designed to make you think deeply and uncover truths that will bring you closer to your truest self. I want to encourage you to read this book with an open mind. Be careful not to get too consumed with judgment thoughts about my personal life events that you allow the divine messages at the core of this book to be missed. Lastly, some of the messages in this book may be repeated in different ways or mentioned more than once. This is to help you grasp it's importance.

Ask yourself: "What fruit am I growing in the garden of my mind?" Because when you realize that thoughts shape your reality, you'll stop waiting for the world to change and start cultivating the life you were always meant to live.

1

Chapter 1: Realizing That You Exist

I grew up in a single parent household, the youngest of four children, which had to be hard on my mother. As a kid, you have no idea what personal difficulties, hurdles and defeats your parents had to overcome alongside sacrifices to ensure safety and security for you growing up. This amount of effort and energy can leave parents drained emotionally, physically and mentally. While we know things that we say and do affect the ones we love; I do not believe that parents are to be fully blamed for how our adult life turns out. They were learning as you are now and deserve grace. By a certain age you've got to be able to acknowledge that you were affected by something, but admit that you have the power to change the course that your life takes.

I could tell you about all of the trauma I've accumulated growing up but I'd like to focus more on my intention to transcend the thoughts of victim-hood. I'd like to support you by stating my realization that we ALL incur trauma. Just as change is inevitable, it is evident that traumatic life experiences are as well. Trauma is a part of our very birthing process and is deeper than surface situations. It is something that is seeping into us as we are baking in our mothers' womb. To explain further, if there is any trauma that our mother has suffered without bringing awareness to, then this trauma gets passed onto us because as humans our behaviors and habits simply mirror our traumas.

Do not get discouraged as you read this, rather keep an open mind. Gaining new information can cause us to become uncomfortable. This is because our subconscious mind has a job to protect all that we are and the current information that we know. It may reject any new information that goes against what you were taught to believe which is responsible for the discomfort you feel. However, adapting a new set of beliefs is what assists us in shifting our paradigms (a model or pattern that make up our programming and habits). In case no one has told you yet, it is definitely okay to adopt new beliefs.

I want to express how important mental health is and that it should be a norm to be discussed among everyone in your family. In my case, I had never heard of mental health growing up. In fact, I had no idea that a mind could be referred to as being sick or well.

I was on what I like to refer to as "autopilot" up until the age of twenty-one. Never questioning anything; just doing as I was taught at home, in school and from adults. People told me how I should feel and what I should or shouldn't do but rarely explained why or furthermore, asked how I felt about what they wanted me to do. I understand that children are unable to make sound decisions or know what's best for themselves...to an extent, however the turning point is when we become of age and fully capable of doing what's best for ourselves, yet our parents can sometimes have an unnoticed grip on how they want our futures to look without allowing us the space to learn the essence of who we are and what we require to live a balanced and harmonious existence. This is mainly because they themselves experienced the same kind of direction from adults in their lives growing up.

As mentioned above, I was on autopilot until the age of twenty-one. My personal definition of autopilot is defined as being a default creator. I created experiences in my life without being aware of how I was reacting to my thoughts. I hadn't really acknowledged my existence or felt what it meant to be alive. Therefore I fell into a hypnotic rhythm of creating unwanted life situations.

I was an average 21 year old whose days consisted of working at a coffee shop, hanging out with friends, going to bed and waking up to repeat the same cycle. I had no interest in going to college because the rat race didn't make sense to me. I also didn't know who I was, what I truly enjoyed or what field of work my life would benefit from essentially. Repetition felt torturing to me so I quickly got tired of my repeated routine and wanted change, but what I found out next would change my life forever.

For at least two weeks I had been feeling sick with stomach pains, fatigue and had painful swollen breasts and lymph nodes. I continued to go to work because my attendance wasn't the best, neither was my attitude. I was sure to be present at work this day, but I could no longer bear my symptoms. I scurried off to the back office to take a quick break and began to cry. My office manager noticed that I was distracted and not my usual self. She asked if everything was okay. I undermined what I truly felt and told her I was just in a little pain. I let her know that I hadn't been feeling good for quite some time and although she wasn't a big fan of mine, She said to me "work isn't as important as your health, I'm going to call an ambulance for you because you really don't look well." When the ambulance arrived, I was embarrassed that I was causing such a scene and that all of my co-workers and our customers witnessed me being strapped to a gurney and hauled off in an ambulance.

When I arrived at the hospital, the doctor examined me and asked questions. He performed blood work and other tests. As I waited for the tests to come back I sat alone in the cold examination room lonely and scared of what the issue could possibly be. Thoughts of a terminal illness, infection, or an STD crossed my mind and I immediately started to pray saying "God if you get me out of this one, I promise I will change my ways." I kept everything to myself because I didn't trust anyone to tell what I was going through. I felt like others would perceive me as someone who wasn't "strong". It had appeared to me that someone who was strong kept everything to themselves. Someone who was strong went through things alone and eventually they'd make it through.

The doctor came back into the room and asked me "do you know that you are pregnant?" I shockingly replied "no". My mind replayed the scene a few days earlier when my mother asked me if I was pregnant, but I was certain that such a thing couldn't happen to me. In my mind, I was not one of those young girls who got pregnant before she had made anything of herself although I was not as careful in my sex acts as I could be. In fact, I never thought "what if I get pregnant?" I knew I was not ready for a child because I barely could care for myself and the thought of bringing a baby to the environment I lived in was gut wrenching. All I could do was stare blankly, thinking to myself "I guess I am the girl who was pregnant without a clear vision of how I wanted my future to look." I could only think about how I would ruin this child's life and force it to become another statistic. Given the emotional and physical abandonment, verbal abuse and other trauma I had experienced; I couldn't imagine bringing a child into this cruel world and definitely not in this home.

"Angel, Angel..." The doctor said tapping my leg. Both in shock and tears, I replied with a shaky voice "yes?", "I would like to discuss your options with you" he said. Before he could tell me, I wailed and blurted out "I can't have this baby". I opted to terminate the pregnancy. I didn't think about my options nor did I discuss it with anyone close to me due to fear of judgment and lack of support. I only knew that chaos was happening inside and outside of me. Aside from me not being sure who the father was, I also knew whichever guy it was, would not truly want to be a father to a child of mine.

The procedure was scheduled. At this point, a pill was not an option. Sad to say, I was too far along. This truly made my decision harder because although it was what I absolutely felt needed to be done, what a terrible way to do it. Realistically there was no right way to do what felt harsh. The only way I was able to get through it was to disallow myself to feel. I went numb.

When I arrived at the center, there were a few other women there. Although we were all there for the same thing, I was embarrassed to be there. I walked up to the front desk, checked in and sat down looking at the floor while twiddling my fingers until my name was called. "Angel!" said the nurse calling out for me. My stomach dropped to the floor as if I was on a roller coaster going down a huge drop. I looked up and realized that my best friend's sister was the nurse admitting me. All kinds of thoughts ran through my head about everyone in the neighborhood knowing my business. However, once we were privately in a room, she assured me that she would never tell anyone and that if she did she could lose her job.

When I got back to the procedure room, the last thing I recall before being put under sedation was the nurses explaining the procedure and asking me to count backwards from five.

When it was all said and done, they gave me feminine pads to put on and sent me to triage for one hour to watch my recovery. Tears streamed down my face. Whatever numbness I had physically and emotionally began to thaw. After being discharged, I cried walking to the bus stop and on the bus going home. When I got home, I wiped my face as if nothing was wrong, went quickly to my room, closed the door and continued to cry as a I curled up into a fetal ball.

This led to a deep depression. I felt all alone and like no one would care. After all, how could anyone be there for me when I had committed such a horrible act? What made it worse was

CHAPTER 1: REALIZING THAT YOU EXIST

having the sonogram pre-procedure. I held the picture and laid in bed sobbing until I fell asleep.

The depression lasted months. My room was terribly dirty. I gained a lot of weight and I called out of work very often. My mother noticed I wasn't myself. She asked if I was okay. I surrendered…sobbing and telling her what I went through and showing her the ultrasound image. She hugged me and asked me why I didn't tell her. Our relationship wasn't close, so opening up to her felt foreign but freeing. She gave me an embrace that I had longed for and told me that having the picture probably wasn't a good idea and that I needed to let it go so that I could heal.

I remember laying in my bed for several days in silence but reflecting on what led to all of this. I'd remembered the saying that was something along the lines of once you hit rock bottom the only way to go was up. I questioned why I was irresponsibly sexually active. Why I didn't value myself more and what I wanted to achieve before ever considering having children. I got up out of the bed, looked in the mirror and said to myself "this pity party ends now, what are you going to do about this?" My mind couldn't comprehend how I went from feeling victimized to quickly empowered. I just knew I would not let the unborn child and this experience be in vain. I had to be prepared if this situation happened again although I wasn't planning on it.

It'd been the pain and suffering from this situation that awakened me and birthed a meaningful purpose in my life. It was the first time I realized that I existed. It was the first time I realized that I could think for myself and that curiosity was a good thing. A flow of questions started to fill my head as to begin assembling the depth of my personal truths. I read once that if you ask yourself a question, that you are powerful enough to come up with an answer. And so as the answers came flooding in, so did solutions.

My next step was to seek understanding of what I went through in regards to the unresolved traumas like having an inconsistent father and not having the mother-daughter bond I had longed for. I wondered how it affected me. I began studying mental health. I wanted to know what drove some human behaviors. I became more observant of others, their reactions, responses and body language in social settings. I became interested in hearing stories from others about their lives and things they'd overcome. My curiosity was piqued from how many different perspectives of life there was and mostly that negativity was a mindset. It was mind blowing how one new and unfamiliar thought opens the door to a wide range of information and even further a possibility to improve the condition of one's livelihood.

This is the reason why I shared intimate details of my life events because I want you the reader to witness how powerful transparency and vulnerability is when you are fostering personal growth. Vulnerability and transparency promotes emotional processing and resilience. This will be discussed more in depth in chapter three.

A rather creative idea had emerged birthing purpose from my pain. A voice spoke that told me to create a Non-Profit Organization targeting isolation, loneliness and boredom within the youths in my community. It even gave me the name for it. I begin jotting down notes and organizing concepts that came to me. I still had moments of sadness, regret and shame, so when I felt ready, I would start pursuing this idea.

I set out into the neighborhood to meet others who had common goals in mind. Previously, I had no physical example or experience with networking or business but I was failing my way forward and getting the answers and resources that I needed. I had mostly shifted my paradigm and focus to become obsessed with my end goal which was to eventually get into schools to speak with teens, hold informational events about self-awareness and become the go-to organization in the community. This was big for me; no, this was bigger than me. Sometimes I found myself thinking that it was too big a project to take on. The events leading up to this breakthrough helped me feel that I was alive. I realized that prior to, I hadn't barely acknowledged God, myself, nor had I ever known that my life...that everyone's life has an innate purpose.

Self Awareness

Self awareness is the soil where transformation begins. Through every season of growth, we move through layers of understanding- from awakening to alignment, from reflection to peace. Each level reveals something new about who we are and how we grow. In my journey, these five levels became the rhythm of my becoming- the stages that shaped the Fruit of My Thoughts.

This chapter discusses realizing that you exist. This is the *first*

level of awareness; the spark of consciousness. It's when you first notice that your life, your feelings, and your thoughts are yours. You begin to ask, **who am I? Why do I think this way?** You're planting the seed of awareness; it's fragile, but it's the beginning of growth.

The Victim Mentality

A victim mentality isn't just the belief that life keeps happening to you. It's the unconscious agreement to see yourself as powerless, to let your wounds call the shots, and to respond to the world from a place of limitation instead of possibility. When you live this way, your identity becomes shaped by what hurt you. Your story gets stuck on the chapters where life disappointed you. You begin to rehearse the same thoughts and emotions over and over until they feel like truth. But the detriment is subtle; the longer you live from that place, the more you forget that you exist beyond your wounds. You forget you have authorship. You forget you have agency. You forget you have the right -and the responsibility to see yourself as more than what you've survived.

The pain body and somatic awareness

The accumulation of emotional pain, unprocessed memories, old stories, and reactive patterns is what rises up when you are triggered. It's the version of you that still believes the past is happening right now. It speaks in fear, in defensiveness, in self-doubt, in anger, in shutdowns. And if you don't realize that you exist separately from your pain body, you'll think it's voice is your own. You'll think the victim narrative is you. You'll think the worst thoughts are you. You'll think the old wounds are still your identity. Further, the pain body (a term coined by Eckhart Tolle, author of "the power of now") is not just a term, it speaks to the truth that emotional pain that isn't addressed can manifest as physical dis-ease.

But the awakening- the moment you realize you exist is the moment you can observe those internal reactions and say: ***"that's not me. That's my pain speaking."*** This awareness breaks the cycle. It pulls you out of unconscious survival mode and places you back in the seat of your own consciousness. Suddenly, you can see the difference between your true self and the pain body that has been steering your life in the dark. And in that moment, you understand the real detriment of a victim mentality; it blinds you from discovering the self that has been there all along- the self that thinks, chooses, creates and transforms.

For years, I didn't realize that my nervous system was living in constant alert mode. Even the smallest shifts felt like threats. Awakening taught me to slow down and notice the tension behind my thoughts. I had to teach my body that it is finally safe through breathing deeper, resting on purpose, and letting myself pause without guilt. When my body softened, my mind began to soften too.

Realizing that you exist is the first step toward reclaiming that self. It is the doorway out of the pain body and into your personal power. It is the moment the fruit of your thoughts begin to grow something new.

Action Step

Write down the experience you had that completely changed or could've changed your perspective of life? What was the moment that took you off of autopilot and made you intentional?

Instilled thinking & inner child awareness

Thoughts can be borrowed, shared and adopted. I felt this important to mention because in the beginning of my story, I talked a little about my childhood upbringing and mental health and I want to be sure that readers understand the entirety of not only how thoughts affect us but where they originate from sometimes. Habits and patterns begin forming from the time you are brought into this world. It is safe to assume that the unhealthy habits our parents have usually get passed down to us. Children mock what they see, so if they see mommy eating all day, they want to eat with her, then they grow up eating all day because that is what they are used to. The importance to changing the negative habits or beliefs that you have is to first understand where it originated. Was this a thought that came from you, or was this something you were taught to believe as a truth? Aside from that our minds don't usually deviate from what we see with our eyes, therefore we began to know this as a personalized truth.

When I began acknowledging my inner child, I realized I wasn't broken, I was responding with a heart that had not yet been healed. I had to understand that awareness wasn't just about observing myself, it was about embracing myself. This was the moment I learned that healing requires holding the hand of the child you used to be.

Action Step

What are your deepest feelings about who you are, the habits that you have and the efforts that you perform?

Personal Power

Personal power is the power you hold as an individual. It is the ability to realize that you are allowed to have emotions, all the while, having the ability to react in a sound way that will benefit you and anyone surrounding you in the long run. When personal power is coupled with positive intent, it will without a doubt produce life changing results. You are careful not to act in a harmful and resentful manner that will trigger a rhythm of alike responses. I want to bring to your attention that with every phase of the discussed predicament, resolution and action plan, my thoughts supported each. My thoughts supported my stagnation, fears, depression yet also my thoughts supported my decision to make the best out of what had happened by adhering to ideas that encouraged me to overcome my dealings. I also want to bring to your attention that I chose the positive thoughts, as there were many others in the negative direction that I could have chosen. Not only did this situation give me the space to heal an aspect of me that I didn't know needed healing before, it introduced opportunities for me to thrive and help others.

Readers might ask what the difference is between having personal power and being controlling is, and I want to make it clear that personal power is exercising the power that you have over your life; more deeply the power that you have over your mindset, reaction, and perception. Being fixated on controlling all outcomes in your life would suggest that you are trying to have power over others. There isn't a situation or struggle that we have personally that isn't a result of our direct contact with another person. I am not suggesting the removal of self accountability, I am pinpointing that when perspectives clash and self-awareness is absent in one or both individuals involved, you get a testy drawback that can leave a dent on your self-esteem and character.

Intention

Intention is an aim or a plan. With every action or reaction to a situation, our reasoning is the bottom line and will dictate the situation's end result. Having a clear intention helps you keep sight of your personal power. If we use my story as an example, my intention to not let my experience be in vain served as the foundational intent to harness my personal power thus producing a self empowered outcome. If I had chosen to stay disgruntled about my situation, I would have given away my personal power to negative intent. It's helpful when we can make a decision with the end goal in mind and consider how we'd in sum be affecting ourselves and our loved ones in the long run.

The first identity shift

The first shift is uncomfortable because you feel caught between two selves; who you were and who you're becoming. You sense something awakening but you can't explain it. Old thoughts don't feel right anymore. Old environments drain you. Old habits irritate your spirit. It's the moment you realize: "I cannot unknown what I now know and see."

2

Chapter 2: Hurting From Reverting

In chapter one, I told readers that I got the creative idea to start a Non-Profit Organization. I also told readers that I had no knowledge of business and networking. I had set out into the community with sheer will and passion pursuing a photo shoot for the youth. My vision entailed kids of a specific age range wearing costumes of who they envisioned themselves to be in the future or creating posters with personable messages on it that would instill in viewers that they were not alone in whatever it was they felt lacked in their lives as to promote that we all have a story someone can relate to. I sat down and started building a team for this project. I believed we were going to mastermind this vision and see it through. Then one individual I met with informed me that I could not move forward with this idea of claiming to have a Non-profit organization without having filed proper paperwork. He said I could potentially get into trouble from the government and the city for "soliciting." How could I forget to do my research on this?

When I finally did the research, all of the paperwork required

CHAPTER 2: HURTING FROM REVERTING

confused me and the fees were more than I could afford or, at least that's what my mind had believed at the time. Ultimately I was discouraged and all of the negative mental chatter didn't help. I was prepared only for things to go the way I wanted them to. But Because I had an expectation that did not pan out, I reverted back to my old ways of allowing my negative thoughts to make my important decisions.

On another note, everything hadn't gone sour. One thing I realized about myself was that my work ethic improved. Although I had reverted back to my old thinking in many ways, I didn't have an attitude with the world about how my life was anymore. In fact, the least I could do was make a positive impact on people I came in contact with day to day. Having a pleasing personality gave me a temporary fulfillment because when I went home and had nothing else to keep my mind busy, it quickly filled with negative thoughts about who I was and what I couldn't accomplish. I again felt like the lonely girl whom no one understood and could relate to.

An unhealthy habit I possessed was utilizing sexual intercourse to mask the abandonment issues I had. I didn't have a significant other because I didn't feel worthy of one, so these were casual hook-ups. It was a habit I continued even after my unplanned pregnancy but this time around I was more mindful that pregnancy could happen, so I lessened the frequency of my habit and made sure that I dealt with one person intimately at a time. That was progress for me.

Some days I felt like I was being punished for my decisions and not figuring out how to legalize my Nonprofit especially when I started feeling sharp aches and pains in my abdomen. At first I believed the pains were a result of my menstrual cycle approaching, but as the days went on the pains got worse. The aches grew rapidly. The fear of possibly being pregnant again and having a miscarriage crippled me so I avoided the doctor and hoped the pain would go away on its own.

The very next day the pain was so excruciating that it brought me to my knees and all I could do was scream in agony. I cried out for my mother. She ran into my room shouting "what's wrong?! What's wrong?!" I asked her to call an ambulance. I could barely talk to explain what I felt or walk to get myself dressed. My mother urged them to hurry yelling frantically on the phone. When the ambulance arrived, I had broken out in a cold clammy sweat, and my pulse was weak and thready. I felt like my life was abruptly coming to an end. While I was being put into the ambulance I blacked out from the pain. I was in and out of consciousness. My mother tapped my face worriedly saying "Angel please keep your eyes open". She was petrified.

When we arrived at the hospital I was barely coherent, but I remember the nurses asking me what happened and what was wrong. The only thing I could do was scream and cry. They quickly administered medicine that soon eased the pain. I had never been so in pain in my life and had no idea what was wrong. The only thing I could think was that I deserved this because of my previous actions.

My hospital stay was 7 days long. At first, the doctors had determined it an "unknown etiology". Two days later, the doctor diagnosed me with Mesenteric Adenitis, a disorder that causes lymph nodes in the abdomen to become inflamed and swollen. I was relieved to find out that this wasn't what I thought it was. The next day after further tests were run, I was told that the wrong diagnosis was given. My actual diagnosis was Pelvic Inflammatory Disease which was caused by a curable STD that I had for an extended period of time without treating. The bacteria from the STD had spread and infected my womb, ovaries and Fallopian tubes. The doctor explained to me that the disease is curable and that it should clear up in a few weeks with treatment. He also mentioned that the disease caused scar tissue in my uterus which would make my chances of having a child in the future slim to none. I felt that this was only confirmation of my punishment.

After receiving medications I started feeling better, yet sad that the option for me to have children in the future was taken away from me. Eventually I accepted this "punishment" as my reality. At this point, the universe had made it clear to me that I needed to continue working on the things within my control. It was time for me to address my feelings of abandonment and loneliness. What better place to contemplate my decisions and what I had just encountered than a hospital.

Once I was released from the hospital, I wanted to make changes effective immediately. I started by deleting the numbers of the guys that I hooked up with and limiting certain "friends" access to me. I vowed to myself that I would become celibate to focus on building my relationship with myself and God. I knew this would be challenging.

The second thing I did was look for positive ways to express myself and to release whatever sadness or negativity that would arise on my journey without fear of anyone judging me. I joined a local church and consistently showed up every Sunday and for special church events to stay encouraged. On a scientific level **I was creating new neural pathways.**

Before I knew it, I was six months into my celibacy and feeling extremely proud of myself. My confidence grew and my thoughts grew more positive with it. Still an employee at the coffee shop, I longed for something different. After all, I was going on year five of working the same occupation. I loved my job and it assisted me in my transition of providing a more pleasant attitude to not only customers, but individuals I came in contact with in everyday life. However, I was intentional with growing in all areas of my life and the promotion I craved hadn't happened. Maybe that was a sign that it was time for me to move on. I wanted to shed my old mindset, surroundings, and situations to make room for new ones. Out with the old, in with the new.

As I was sitting in my room after working a long shift, I pulled my phone out and scrolled through social media posts. One specific post caught my attention. It was that of a close friend's brother who was consistently in trouble with the law. This specific post surprised me because it showed him sitting at a desk, wearing a suit and tie in an office setting as he spoke about transforming his mind and habits. He urged others to join a network marketing venture he had embarked upon and appeared to be having success with. This piqued my curiosity so I reached out to him compelled to hear his story of transformation. If it sounded legit, only then did I want to hear more about this business venture. I was searching to gain education on how to become a business owner. Furthermore, I wanted to do something new, exciting and challenging. This could potentially be the first test for my renewed mindset. This time I'd be aware enough not to allow my expectation and fear to get the best of me if something didn't go my way. I reached out to him and set up a time and day to meet at his office.

The day of the meeting arrived. Although this was my close friends' brother, I never really knew him in depth and also wasn't sure who he had known at this point. I wanted to look the part so I put on my best professional outfit and headed out the door. When I arrived, we greeted one another and walked down the hall to his office. The office had two parts and was painted green and white. Informative pictures of the product he sold were hung up on the walls. There were stacked chairs, a six foot table and a white dry erase board embedded in the wall that appeared to be used for meetings and planning. We walked through this room to a more private portion of the two-part office. In this room, there were two glass circle tables, side-by-side with desk chairs. The tables had books on them. It looked as if he had been working on some things before I arrived. There were also two tall file cabinets. This room was a bit smaller than the other but still a nice sized office. The room was aromatic with scents of lavender and jazz music played softly in the background.

"Welcome! Here have a seat" Robert said as he pulled out my chair which was in front of his desk. "Thanks!" I replied. Robert took his seat and began to tell me about his experience in prison. He went on to explain to me that he was very intelligent but had used all he knew in the wrong ways. He told me that after he got out of prison, he met a man while working at a supermarket who had told him about the business. As he was telling me more, the man walked in. "Mr. Jones! I was just telling Angel how we met." Robert said. Mr. Jones was his up-line...further explaining that an up-line is the person that recruited you into the Multi-Level marketing business. Mr. Jones chimed in on our conversation, introducing himself and continuing the story about how they met. He edified Robert while telling me about the company values, how many lives they changed, the conferences, compensation plan and more.

Mr. Jones made samples of the product for me to try. When I learned that the products were coffee and tea, I was charged up. I had worked at a coffee shop for five years so I knew coffee like the back of my hand and was confident that I could sell and recruit with this product. "This desk beside me is yours if you're ready to join the team" said Robert. What a way to close the pitch! I had never been this excited in my life! Is this what sheer focus. willpower and longing for more could bring me? I never saw this coming. In fact, I hadn't imagined in a million years that I could become a business owner. I was sold on the concept of the business and signed up with my investment on the product with Robert as my up-line.

The next week Robert and Mr. Jones brought me to a company meeting. It was held at an event space in the Bronx, NY. When we arrived the event had already started and I had never seen so many happy and excited people in my life. The song, "Happy" by Pharrell was the theme song at the event and boy were those people happy to be there. The energy was contagious so I joined in the celebration; clapping my hands all the way to my seat.

CHAPTER 2: HURTING FROM REVERTING

At the meeting, I met the rest of our team (those who were overachievers and making over 10k in the business). The event started off with the host being a guy named Frederique who was up-line to a team bringing in 50k and more in revenue a month. He introduced himself and told his story about what made him join the company, then he began to introduce some of his team members who were pulling big numbers in sales and sign-ups. They were awarded and acknowledged for their efforts. Some of the stories told by these individuals were really moving and further confirmed my want to join this company. Although I knew it'd be a learning experience and a way to make money, I had no idea how much work and personal growth it would take to make this possible. All I knew was that I was ready and eager to learn.

It took about two weeks for my products to arrive. Before it got here, I claimed my new desk space at my shared office. I decorated my space with encouraging words. Positive, optimistic, and exciting thoughts filled my brain. I smiled ear to ear. This was the change in my surroundings that I needed. I started creating a hot and cold list of prospects I could potentially have as customers and recruits. I shadowed Robert as he worked and we watched videos about the products. The challenging part was understanding the compensation plan. However my excitement to recruit and sell carried me through the hurdles in my mind. I was completely engulfed in my business and my hunger for knowledge grew immensely.

A book that I was encouraged to read before I set out recruiting was "Think and Grow Rich" by Napoleon Hill. This book confirmed I was on the right track in my thinking to continue producing positive thoughts and images about what I wanted for myself and the woman I was working to become. Eventually, I became a bookworm, reading books and listening to the audios. My studies included psychology and how to build multiple streams of income. I was stunned that all of this valuable information had never been taught to those around me. I thought to myself that someone's got to teach this to them and that once I had applied these things to my life, I could lead by example and teach others.

Business had been moving slow and I sometimes grew frustrated with how many people were close minded about the idea of becoming an independent business owner. I did presentations for family members, strangers and friends. It'd been one month and I hadn't recruited anyone yet. I was hard on myself. It wasn't going as easy as I had expected it to but with my new findings about the complexity of the mind, it made sense for me to work towards detaching from the "no's." This business required a lot of mental work. I had to find a way to insert a healthy balance of work and restful reflection into my day. As a new routine, I went into the office early to meditate before starting work. If I was having a rough day, I'd paused to meditate and collect my thoughts before doing anything more. Eventually, I had managed to get my product into two local stores on consignment deals and business started to pick up.

My mindset was steady to improve and many of the things I allowed and entertained in the past were no longer welcome in my presence. Most of the friendships and relationships I had became distant. To give you a clear understanding, my past life didn't only consist of having unprotected sex. It also included fighting and binge drinking, so you could imagine my transformation left some people surprised, unimpressed, and even angry. I didn't care that no one mentioned being proud of me. How they felt was none of my business and I understood how projection worked from the self-taught studies of psychology. I became "unrecognizable" to others but to me I was transformed by the renewal of my mindset.

Myself along with Robert and other colleagues of ours decided to start a group called "The Go-To Network" to help grow exposure to our businesses and build lasting connections. The GTN was created to encourage networking, togetherness and collaboration within the contacts in the group. The group would be made up of a mixture of businesses and professionals in various fields of studies. If anyone needed anything, we'd provide a referral to the business or professional that could assist most with the need. We held our first event at a local event space which had agreed to sponsor all of our upcoming and future events.

Among those that attended the event was Mr. Fair. He was the proud owner of a non-profit organization dedicated to the youths and was very active in the community. He had contacts in high places. I was filled with excitement as I spoke with him about the experience with my failed attempt to start the Nonprofit because I knew that he was educated on the pieces missing to my puzzle. He gave me a number for someone who specialized in filing paperwork for organizations. All I could think to myself was "when the student is ready, the teacher shall appear."

Mr. Fair became my mentor and taught me everything I needed to know about having a Nonprofit Organization. I volunteered with his mission while in the process of awaiting my paperwork completion. It took roughly three months to complete. In the midst, we went on field trips, had events to educate about money management, delivered presents to children at Christmas time and more. I was proud of the woman I had become- teachable, aware, giving and fearless.

My non-profit paperwork was finally finished and it was time for me to get to work on my vision utilizing all of the information and skills Mr. Fair had taught me. I continued to work my business but my focus naturally began to shift more towards making a difference for the youth within my community.

Reflection

Reflection is the bridge between simply noticing your inner landscape and beginning to understand it. If the first level of self-awareness is realization, the moment you awaken to the fact that your thoughts, patterns and emotions exist, then reflection is the second level of self- awareness; a gentle, conscious act of turning toward what you've noticed and observing it with intention.

Reflection requires stillness, honesty, and willingness. It's not about fixing anything, it's about understanding the roots beneath the fruit your thoughts produce. Reflection is the point where you begin to see cause and effect in your inner world. With reflecting, you no longer project blame, you observe your part in your own emotional cycles. Reflection is where emotional responsibility begins.

Reflection Vs Rumination

Reflection is conscious observation, while rumination is unconscious looping. Rumination keeps you stuck while reflection moves you forward. Reflection sounds like; "Let me understand this so I can grow." Rumination sounds like: "I can't believe this happened, why me!?" It is through reflection that the pain body becomes visible, giving you access to healing rather than suppression.

Action Step

Write down a time when you reverted back to an old habit. What thoughts do you think encouraged you to revert? How did or will you get back on track with your positive thoughts? What do you feel you should let go off in order to get back on track? What new habits have you formed that support positive thinking and changed behavior?

Negativity Bias

Negativity bias subtly pulls you backward by over highlighting old wounds because even when you are changing, your mind can drag you back to memories that reinforce old identities. Statements or thoughts like: "I always mess up. Why even try" are markers for the negatively biased mind. Growth can feel unsafe because the brain pays more attention to the discomfort of the unfamiliar than the reward of the future. The mind mistakenly believes the old patterns; avoidance, shutdown, self-doubt- are safer because they're known, so reverting becomes the default reaction, not a conscious choice.

The pain you feel from reverting isn't just from 'falling back.' It's the internal conflict between the new you trying to emerge and the old mind fighting to keep you predictable and protected. Negativity bias often amplifies that inner battle, making setbacks feel like proof you haven't changed even when you actually have.

Creating New Habits

In this chapter, I spoke about creating new neural pathways in my mind, so I want to give you a scientific perspective about how new habits are formed. A neural pathway is a series of connected nerves along which electrical impulses travel in the body. The neurons and dendrites that a neural pathway is composed of are created in the brain with each habit and behavior. Think of the kids movie "Inside Out" if you will. The islands of personality that were created for the character Riley were symbolic of the process of habit formation. Though they were primarily portrayed as emotional and identity- based structures, they share striking parallels with how habits are built reinforced, and sometimes reshaped.

Our brain cells communicate with each other through a process known as "neuronal firing". When brain cells exchange information often, the connection between them strengthens. Therefore the messages that travel the same pathways continuously, help to create repetition which then forms automatically, creating habit. Awareness is healing and when we know the process of how something works, it aids us in understanding why we may deviate from the information we learned. Ultimately you will find that comfort zones and fear both are primary factors in the act of deviating.

Let's unpack in depth why we tend to revert back to old habits. The human brain is widely complex and has what is known as the subconscious mind. The subconscious mind houses our beliefs, emotions, creativity, long-term memory, intuition and values. It's job is to act as a bridge between it and the conscious mind by utilizing the habits, information and beliefs that you were taught to make things run smoothly. It is responsible for protecting the informational processes of the things you endured from the time you were a baby by storing it to create the reality and personality you have today. Scientific studies suggest that the subconscious mind can be accessed through self awareness, conscious presence, and other techniques like hypnosis and dream analysis to explore its hidden layers.

Because the subconscious mind is is responsible for a wide array of functions that are crucial for everyday life, it is imperative that I bring to your awareness that you can adopt a new set of beliefs, values and all of the things I mentioned are housed in the subconscious mind. The subconscious mind does not know the difference between right or wrong nor does it recognize time. It will adopt any idea, thought or vision that you imprint upon it. Therefore, we should be cautious of the things we allow access to through our five senses on a day to day basis. Even further, it should be freeing to know that with your thinking, actions, visualization and emotional intelligence, you can create a life that you long for.

When we want to introduce a new habit, the subconscious mind kicks in sending out thoughts of fear which can physically manifest as procrastination, lack of confidence, and inconsistency. This happens because as mentioned earlier, the subconscious mind is working to protect the habit that you are trying to replace with one that is unfamiliar. When we are not aware of this, we tend to go back to what we already know and what is comfortable. Anything that is troubling you, research it, ask questions about it and when you gain a newfound awareness, you will find that it will be hard for your mind and body to function in any knowing less than the new one that is supporting and sufficient for your growth on all levels. If you don't believe me, you can certainly put this theory to test.

Re-building self-trust

Every time I reverted, I questioned my progress. But self-trust is rebuilt the same way it was lost...one small moment at a time. Acts like keeping your word to yourself, saying "no' when something drains you, choosing rest before burnout, and showing up when you're afraid are all ways to re-build self trust. Self trust grows every time you honor who you're becoming instead of who you used to be.

Boundaries

Boundaries are not walls. They are doors you learn to close gently but firmly. When I began setting boundaries, I realized

I wasn't protecting myself from others; I was protecting the version of me I was working so hard to become. Boundaries are a love language with yourself. They are proof of growth.

Faith without works is dead

In this chapter, I wanted change and just hoping for it wasn't going to get me it. I had to align my actions with what I wanted. My actions being joining a church, becoming celibate, starting a business and going the extra mile with community outreach all contributed to me learning new strengths about myself and kept me from seeking fulfillment in the wrong ways. I replaced bad habits with good ones. In my opinion prayer is an action word and when we work towards what we want, we continue to show the God that we are deserving of it, that it is ours. Lastly, pray, but do it in your own way. Thank God for things you want as if you already have them because again, the subconscious mind cannot tell what is reality or fiction. It is as if you have to assume the role of who you want to be in that very present moment to continue turning the knobs of physical manifestation and once you do that, well its safe to say that how you want to be is exactly who you are.

Action Step

Write down in what areas of your life you lack faith? Draw out the emotion that promotes your lack of faith towards this. Whatever emotion or feeling that is drawn out from this action step, will need to be consciously addressed, then replaced with new strategies of positive self-talk.

"When the student is ready, the teacher shall appear"

This saying refers to readiness. Sometimes we think we are ready to take on a task and then the minute something happens outside of our control, we are ready to give it all up. Take my situation regarding having proper paperwork for my organization for instance. The only thing I was ready to do was start, however lack of information, impatience and disorganization are all signs of not being ready. We can combat this by learning as much as we can about the very thing we want to do and as we implement focusing on the things we want to attain, we'll meet people who help us get even further. When we meet new people the very thing that helps us is the knowledge or resources they share with us. When we explore the resources they too contain useful information. In short, your journey depends deeply on the knowledge and resources you'll acquire. Be sure to keep an open mind and remain ready and focused so that you don't miss them.

Action Step

Write down the areas of your life you'd like to flourish in, what is missing for you? How prepared are you? How can you get more prepared?

A coincidence? No, synchronicity!: The definition of coincidence is a random or chance occurrence without a perceived deeper meaning. But when we experience synchronicity (a term created by psychiatrist and analytical psychologist Carl Jung) which transcends the depth of coincidence, it feels more significant, purposeful and in alignment with our personal states. Recognizing this can help you become more intentional about what you believe to be true and how you how you feel about your life events.

Grace for the process

Reverting brought guilt but healing teaches grace. You are allowed to not get it right every time. You are allowed to grow at your own speed. You are allowed to try again. Grace makes room for transformation. It gives you permission to rise without shame.

Action Step

Let's end the action steps for this chapter by summoning the feeling of gratitude. Write down a synchronicity that you can pinpoint in your life; The something that felt deeper than a coincidence. How did it make you feel?

3

Chapter 3: Harvest Season

The seed I had sown years ago for my non profit organization and personal growth was beginning to sprout. It's germination was the awareness I practiced and the direction and mentorship I received from Mr. Fair. Now that we had our legal paperwork, it was time to start planning an event. One where we could make our introduction to the community while doing the very thing we were created to do- promote self awareness, healing and unity. I had based my organization off of my so-far life experiences and utilized the knowledge, steps and information I had gained along the way to create the events, activities and mentorship that would take place within the organization. It was time to execute the plans I had for my vision.

I was ready to transparently tell my story. I had no fears because I knew that if I wanted to be a vessel of God that I would need to embrace vulnerability to encourage it within the community and also to inspire others. Being disciplined in what I believed in was so important to me. Therefore, I had to set boundaries with loved ones who viewed me in the light of my old self and talked down on me when I shared that I'd tell my story.

Y.W.E.S stood for Young women's empowerment seminar which was my idea for my first event. I connected with six young women within the community who were doing amazing things and added them as panelists with an older adult overachiever as the keynote speaker to tie the message altogether. It had been my vision to celebrate them in all the greatness that they were doing but also to strategically throw discussions in the mix that provoked thought for them and the audience; questions that raised awareness and would leave everyone with no choice but to think deeply about their life decisions and how we treat others. My approach could be compared to that of a masseuse who massages the external parts of the body but targets deep tissues to work out the kinks.

We had a packed event with over 50 attendees. I expected people to show up but not to the extent of there being no seats left leaving some attendees to stand. I was blown away that people were willing to support something that had only started off as a vision in my mind's eye. Other than giving presentations for 2 to 3 potential prospects at a time while in network marketing, I had no prior speaking experience and definitely not any in front of this many people. This would be my first event as a transformational speaker and it was a full house. What a way to step into my calling, feeling fully supported by my community. The seminar lasted about two hours. We laughed, we cried, we celebrated, and we expressed gratitude. It became a safe space for all of those in attendance.

After it was over, there were individuals waiting their turn to talk with me about how they were positively impacted, how they wanted to be involved in the next event, or how they were proud of my transformation. I was only being my authentic self, therefore I wasn't sure how to fully receive all of the praise and positive feedback I was getting.

I went on to do 5 more seminars in the near future, adding 3 Y.M.E.S (Young Men's Empowerment Seminars) so that the men in the community could also be empowered. The seminars were amazing and it was time to expand our reach. I had gained the courage to submit a proposal to present a mini empowerment seminar at my old high school. If there was anything I needed or wanted to know about business, I did research and asked questions. I had learned about creating proposals for different things. The more I did for my organization, the more I learned. I was excited and my confidence reflected that.

With the help of one of my former varsity basketball coaches, the proposed offer was accepted and the date was set. I reached out to all of the panelists who were a part of my previous empowerment seminars and asked if they'd join me. I felt that the kids would be more receptive to what we had to say because we were closer in age to them (our ages ranged from 23-25). A group of about 7 of us met up in a park across the street from the high school so that we could walk into the school together. I felt a bit nervous but eventually it subsided as the support I felt from my peers overpowered the nervousness. I had thoughts that the students would think we were boring, or that they would be rowdy, unsettled and inattentive.

When we entered the school auditorium, the students sat watching us enter. Some were slouched with their arms crossed, others sat upright and attentive, and others looked anxious and excited to see what we would be talking about. The principal introduced us and warned the kids to behave. I took the floor to introduce myself and inform them about our mission. The goal of the assembly was to encourage the students to practice mindfulness and to educate them on the power of self awareness and embracing the things about themselves that set them apart from others. My approach was to demonstrate transparency and vulnerability just in case any of them experienced similar things as I did along my journey.

I was ecstatic seeing the students receive what we spoke about, participate in the discussion, ask questions and even share a bit of their own thoughts and experiences. It had appeared that they were very open and optimistic during the assembly. At the end we got requests to be mentors and to offer advice and guidance from the students. Several weeks after the assembly, I began receiving emails and texts from students with testimonials on getting tested for STD's or taking their sex life more seriously and being more intentional about caring for their mindsets. That for me was a successful harvest. It was the result of the seeds of faith, action and self-belief that I planted in the previous chapters.

Due to the high request of mentorship from the youth in my community, I decided to take to a local youth center to teach a personal growth and development class to children ages 12 and up with a signed waiver of permission from their parents and the okay from the head of the center. I had created a syllabus to teach to the youth about how to become self aware and why it is so important. My teachings included interactive games, creative writing, vision board parties, and events where guest speakers could come and share stories of inspiration and wisdom. The guest speakers ranged from ex-pro football players to college graduates who were excelling in their respective fields of expertise. The feedback was amazing but most importantly watching some of the kids utilize what they had been taught was even better.

I was proud to be the first young adult in my community to have fostered a positive transformation experience for myself first and then many others. Regardless of the negativity I dealt with at home, or the money I felt that I had lacked at the time, I managed to rise above excuses, victim-hood, and self sabotage. The more I opened up, the more I realized my story wasn't mine alone. When you're open, people don't just celebrate your harvest, they understand your soil. My ability to be seen as I was is what truly built trust and legacy in my community. Vulnerability became my invitation for others to believe they could grow too.

As I looked around at what I had built, I realized the harvest wasn't the end. It was proof that new seasons were waiting beneath the soil. My community didn't just see my success; they saw my becoming. And that connection... the willingness to be real with them was the richest fruit of all.

The harvest taught me that growth is never just about what blooms in the open, it's also about what breaks beneath the surface. Every triumph I've shared with my community carries the fingerprint of silent tears, unseen prayers, and the courage to be transparent even when it wasn't easy. I used to think harvest was the reward for being strong, but I learned that it's the gift of being real. It's what happens when you stop performing perfection and start honoring your process. The soil remembers every truth you plant, and in time, it gives it back multiplied.

Transparency and vulnerability

I want to share with you how important I realized being transparent and vulnerable is. Before this realization, I'd been indirectly taught that telling your truths is weakness. Some individuals tend to "sweep things under the rug" fearing to acknowledge how things made them feel because they felt they had to appear "strong" to others. When we sweep things under the rug, we don't give ourselves a chance to process what we've been through. We in fact hold on to all of the emotions that the trauma caused; again building the pain body and continuing to manifest situations in similarity to it- repeating a viscous cycle of chaos until we have the level of awareness that allows us to process and transmute it to a positive purpose. Transparency is not weakness, it's clarity. It is you refusing to blur your own reflection. Vulnerability is the courage to live without the armor of pretense. Demonstration of both is living from your center which is the essence of alignment.

I want to ask you to clearly and carefully define YOUR definition of the word "strong". On the surface, "strong" often means appearing unshaken, unbothered, or always in control. It's the kind of strength that society praises... the straight spine, steady voice, and "I'm fine" smile. But this version of strength is performative. It's strength built for others to see, not for the self live. People learn to wear strength like armor not because they are unbreakable but because they are afraid of being seen as broken. This kind of "strength" hides the truth, pain, fear, exhaustion and trades authenticity for acceptance. True strength faces pain to grow, seeks alignment with self, protects integrity, operates from freedom and connects through truth.

Action Step

Write down the ways that you could be more transparent and vulnerable. What would more transparency and vulnerability do for you? Write the areas of your life where you try to mask your truths in order to appear strong. The fact that you are thinking about this will bring about enough awareness to invoke the seed of change.

Alignment

Alignment is the point where what you know and what you do finally begin to match. It's the stage where self-awareness matures into intentional living. If realization is you waking up and reflection is you understanding your inner world, then ***alignment is the third level of self-awareness***. Alignment is you choosing to live in integrity with understanding. Harvest season is the perfect home for alignment because alignment is what allows you to finally reap the fruit of your inner work. Alignment is the harmonious relationship between your thoughts, actions, boundaries, intentions, habits, emotional truth and lived behavior. It is the end of contradiction and the beginning of congruence.

Alignment & Discipline

Discipline is the structure that makes alignment sustainable. It is how you choose yourself over and over again, even when it's inconvenient or uncomfortable. Alignment cannot exist without discipline because the ego, the pain body, and old narratives will always try to pull you back into the patterns that feel familiar. Discipline is the muscle that keeps you facing forward.

Mentorship & Community

Harvest often arrives through people- teachers, friends, strangers, or unexpected guides who water your growth. I learned that some breakthroughs don't come through solitude. They come through connection. Mentorship and community showed me what was possible. Community showed me I wasn't alone. Conversations became seeds that blossomed into confidence, clarity, and opportunity. Harvest is never a solo season, it is a shared one.

The Universal Truth- Harvest teaches timing

No matter how eager we are, we cannot rush a harvest. We can nurture, water, and protect, but the growth happens on divine time. This humbles us. It reminds us that even when nothing seems to be happening, life is working beneath the surface. Harvest teaches you patience and that silence doesn't mean stillness, and waiting doesn't mean wasting. Harvest is more than success, its the echo of everything you've survived, tended, and trusted. It's proof that faith, patience, and authenticity always bear fruit; not just in your hands but in your heart.

4

Chapter 4: Living in Full Bloom

There's a certain kind of peace that arrives only after you've faced yourself. Not the peace that comes from life being easy, but from finally being honest about who you are, what you desire and what you're no longer willing to carry. That's the season I stepped into when I moved to another state; not because everything was perfect, but because something inside me whispered "it's time to grow a bigger garden." I was proud of what I had accomplished within my community, but I wanted to challenge my strength and I did it by making a big move ten hours away from home.

Staying where I was born and raised felt confining to my spirit. It made me feel conflicted inside for so many reasons. The most prominent reason was the fact that some of my loved ones had only viewed me as the old version of myself, and so when I'd enforce boundaries that were in alignment with my identity at the time, it usually was disregarded or disrespected. I didn't like the feeling of shrinking myself to make anyone comfortable with themselves. For me, it was important to switch my environment so that it'd be aligned with the woman I was becoming.

A few years prior I had met an aunt for the first time. We kept in touch and talked sometimes. After talking with her over the phone about what I was feeling, we had both decided that it'd be a good idea for me to visit her in Ohio. The trip lasted a week and after experiencing a cleaner quality of air, an uncrowded city, more trees and nature... I had decided that I wanted to make this state my new home. My decision came after weighing the pros and cons of both environments. We all know that the body follows the mind and my thoughts led with what I could accomplish in a new place not just business wise, but for my mental health and wellness. I had to protect what I worked to heal.

I returned home after my short trip. It was then that it dawned on me that I'd be leaving behind all that I started to build with the youth and in my city. It pained me to think of how my mentees and the youth that I'd been working with would be affected but to be honest, I was struggling. I had invested mostly all of my savings into my missions and depleted my energy after trying to help a few people in my life with a positive transformation. As bad as it hurt me to leave behind everything I knew and loved, it hurt me worse to feel maxed out because I knew I deserved to receive just as much as I gave. The lesson that I was learning was that I could not grow fruit without watering the soil.

The day came for me to move to Ohio. It was tearful as I said my goodbyes to my family and friends. I hadn't planned on coming back to visit for a while because I needed time to honor my own being. Part of me shedding the old was me getting rid of almost everything that I owned. I packed a suitcase full of clothes and headed off to the bus depot. The bus ride was ten hours long which gave me time to reflect on all that I experienced good and bad back home. It was bittersweet, but freeing. I leaned my head against the window of the bus and smiled. The ruling feeling was gratitude.

When I arrived back in Ohio, I stepped off the bus and stood aside waiting to grab my suitcase from the suitcase storage area on the bus. The air smelled cool and crisp on that warm June day. It was certainly less people outside than what I was used to in New York. After grabbing my suitcase I headed to the parking area to find my family. My aunt waved her hand and smiled. I hurriedly walked over to her and the car and we embraced and got in the car and drove home. My goal was to get settled in, find a job, and work on getting a place of my own.

I had established a good routine being in a new space. I joined a new gym and began venturing out to nature parks to explore while also being paid to babysit full-time for my aunt while she worked. Things seemed to be going good. After about four months something shifted when I attempted to get information about moving out- from my aunt. Her voice had switched as to go from happy to have me there, to upset that I was looking to move out. She started to talk to me in a condescending tone and often suggested that I would not do well if I went on my own. I instantly began to feel uncomfortable, yet I remained focused on what I needed to do without being disrespectful, dismissive or combative.

As I was outside in the front yard with my little cousins, a middle aged woman and her elderly mother walked by. The middle-aged woman was walking her dog and my little cousin who is autistic approached her mother and began rubbing her face. I always felt that autistic children are closer to God and so when I explained to the woman that he was autistic, we both found it fascinating and observed. We engaged in conversation and she said "my name is Wanda I live up the street by the way." I greeted her back saying "hi Wanda, nice to meet you!" She proceeded to tell me about her mother's age and illness. I had recognized her accent and confirmed that she too was from New York. We had something in common. Wanda walked her dog with her mother everyday. Over time, we exchanged numbers and agreed to hang out.

Wanda and I became close; hanging out, going to the gym together, and talking about events and ideas. It had seemed that my aunt was resenting me more and more although I had expressed wanting to do those same things with her. Things had grew so intense that I mostly avoided her. I had began telling Wanda what was going on and she assured me that I did not deserve to be treated that way, so when my aunt informed me that I didn't fit in with her household and that she was sending me back to NY it was no surprise to Wanda and I. I couldn't go back to NY. For me, that would've been going backwards. I called Wanda to let her know, and she told me to pack my things and come down to her house and we would figure out next steps together. Without causing a scene or bickering, or feeling angry, I packed my things up and headed to Wanda's house without forewarning my aunt. In my eyes, she wanted me gone but I did not have to go the way she intended me to.

When I arrived at Wanda's house, which happened to be on New Year's Eve; she had cooked, had warm blankets and created a welcoming environment. We laughed, danced and took pictures to bring in the holiday. By then, I had decided to look for a local shelter to stay at because although Wanda was welcoming and like family at this point, I did not want to invade her space. It was time for me to grow up. We discussed shelters and she called around the next day to see who had space. She found a shelter that was willing to take me. I stayed one more night at Wanda's house and she drove me to the shelter the next day.

As we walked in the shelter, I began to feel extremely sad, walking with my head to the sky attempting to disguise the tears that began to stream from my face. Reality was dawning on me that I didn't even know how to take a bus here to get around, and that I had no family to turn to, no job; and mostly that I was going to be alone now. I looked over at Wanda and she too had tears streaming from her face. She turned to me and said "I'm sorry you have to go through this but you will get through this and you are not alone. Please call me if you need anything and I will do what I can." We hugged tightly and cried together. Then she said "wipe your tears honey, you don't need to have anyone here see you like this. Be careful who you trust and stay alert." I wiped my tears, thanked her and watched her get in her car and pull off.

I walked up to the desk to check-in. I was in a department of the shelter known as the women's day room. It was where women only, came to to watch television, eat breakfast, wash clothes, and wait in between programs, job hunting, and more. They also had a shower in a separate room and a room that women who were sick or tired from work could rest in. The atmosphere was pretty clean. The advisor had walked me back to a place where I could store my suitcase and advised me to remove anything valuable that I may not have wanted stolen. Then she told me to have a seat in the day room until it was time for mandatory church service. The service was right before dinner every evening at 6p and if you didn't attend the service, you were not allowed to eat dinner. This was the same for lunch.

Before attending the service, cellphones had to be shut off. You were not allowed to take a call after 5:59P. We headed downstairs to the cafeteria which looked similar to that of a school cafeteria. The food was not always great so on nights that it wasn't, I skipped eating. After dinner, we formed a line and walked over to the building next door where we slept and showered. There were about 20-30 women who were also in the shelter. When I looked around, I realized that most of them struggled with alcohol or drug addiction and Post traumatic stress syndrome from chaotic upbringings. Although I felt out of place, I was able to relate in some ways. I pondered about how I could make the best out of this situation.

When we entered the stay area, it was surprisingly very clean. It wasn't what I'd imagined a shelter would look like. I imagined that there would be a cold building with cots everywhere on the floor and people sleeping with coats and old clothing on. Instead, they gave fresh pajamas, socks and necessities. There were beds in different rooms of the building; which looked sort of like a frat house, and more than one shower area. This was something for me to be grateful for. What a relief I felt although on my first night, I slept on a cot on floor in the hallway because all of the beds were taken. The next night and thereafter I slept in a bed.

Rules were strictly enforced with only five minutes allotted for shower time, phones were required to be stored in a zip lock bag and locked up as soon as you entered the stay building, 9p sharp bedtime, 6am wake up time and beds were mandatory to be made up every morning. If you wanted, you could stay later to help clean the rooms and bathrooms for a ticket to attend the buffet style employee lunch, which I did often. During the day, they'd allowed you to eat breakfast in the day room and lounge for an hour thereafter, then they'd close the day room to encourage getting out and finding resources for stability.

The only place I knew how to take the bus to was the gym but luckily it was right down the street from where the shelter was. I remembered that I could go there to work out and take a longer shower before going job hunting. When I got there, I scanned my card and was told that it was inactive. I inquired about discounts for homeless people; wondering if maybe I could get in free just once. I was told that homeless people get a free membership if we get a special signed notice from the workers at the shelter and so I did. I was thankful to re-established my gym routine. I incorporated job searching into my routine and attended work shops and even got clothes from the shelter donation shop to look presentable in case any of the jobs offered me an interview.

The shelter allowed individuals who were not homeless but struggled with affording food to eat there too. About a month into being in the shelter, I met a young girl who informed me of a home health aide agency that was hiring. I retrieved the details from her and talked to an advisor about transportation to get there. It was 25-30 minutes away by bus. I had been informed that they could only provide me with 1 -one-way pass to get there but that I'd have to figure out how to get back. It didn't make sense to me that they wanted you to be so active in a job search, yet they only allowed you a one-way pass per day. However, I knew there wasn't anything that could hold me back from getting there and even though I was unsure about how'd I get back, I had faith that God would provide a way as did with many things in my life thus far.

I searched maps directions and asked around about what bus to take to get there. It turned out that the bus I needed to take had a stop directly in front of the women's day room and let me off just at the corner of the home health-aide agency. All of the signs aligned for me to know that this was the job for me. I walked in confident, knowing I'd get the position and I did.

Next, all who were hired had to attend paid training for the 2 weeks. Once again, I had to figured out how I'd manage to get to and from training until I was paid in two weeks. It was time for me to be transparent with my future bosses and co-workers. I told them that I lived in the shelter and I wouldn't have a way to get back. My co worker said to me "don't worry about it. I'll pick you up and drop you off." I thanked her and asked if I could hug her. The next day, some of my new co-workers and bosses showed up to the shelter with sets of scrubs and a care package containing toiletries and feminine products. It was truly hard for me to think of my situation as being terrible because I felt supported, valued and prayed for.

In the midst of getting a job, I got word of a business club that hosted meetings for entrepreneurs to be able to build and network. Since I hadn't known anyone in the city, I decided to attend a meeting to meet new people, seek opportunities, and become known as a speaker. There was a membership fee due in order to continue to be apart of it but when I shared my story, an entrepreneur had decided to sponsor the cost of my dues for a month. I was grateful and God continued to send me experiences and people to be grateful for. My goal wasn't just to stay busy, it was also to prove how strong, intelligent and resilient I was to myself. It was to prove to myself that with faith, anything is possible.

Alignment was abundant for me, but, I needed to continue showing the universe how grateful I was and that even in this time of uncertainty that I still had my faith. I decided to keep a journal to write in all my positive experiences and if I had a negative experience, I'd look for the good in it. One of the entries included witnessing a woman meet her sobriety goals which caused her a great deal of gratitude, and in that she felt compelled to share those emotions and stories with a select few of us at the shelter. To me, that was special. Another entry included the dinner that the shelter hosted for us on mothers day, which included pampering, gift cards and gifts, music and a comedy show. I was not a mother yet, but they still treated those of us who weren't with the same compassion.

I completed training at work and it was time for me to work with clients. My supervisor, Heather, had a special client for me. The drive to the client was 30-40 minutes away with no bus access. Since she had put me on this case, she volunteered to bring me to and from work every shift and even when my hours grew. I worked up to 50 hours a week sometimes. Part of me working so much was not only to save to get my apartment but also because I enjoyed my client who was a car crash survivor with a traumatic brain injury. Part of my job was helping to train him with learning to walk and talk again. I witnessed miracles almost weekly working with him.

My shelter journey lasted 3 months. with me working the last month and a half. I had saved up enough money to put down a security deposit and first months rent on a place I loved. It was my first apartment and I was thrilled that I afforded one with an extra room. I couldn't imagine what kind of pricing I would've dealt with in the renters market in New York. This was my new home and it was peaceful, spacious, and cozy. Heather helped me find furniture and move in. To me, she was a guardian Angel that came into my life and radiated love. I was used to being the person that did that for others, so it felt good to know that someone cared about me too.

All of the things I experienced in this part of my life signified alignment, even moving into the shelter was alignment because I needed a pit stop in between aligning to get me to my next point. Once I was settled in, I reflected back on my experiences. I still had a burning desire to teach others how to overcome hardships first in their minds so that their physical reality could mirror that. Still apart of the business group, I had decided to start hosting conference calls where I educated viewers on the power of their minds. Each week, I spoke on a new topic that provoked thought. This led to new opportunities such as hosting and creating events.

CHAPTER 4: LIVING IN FULL BLOOM

I loved working in the medical field however being a home health aide was demanding on the body and often times uncomfortable because I had to be in other people's homes. I stumbled upon holistic health practices and began studying them but since I had knowledge about both the holistic and medical approach, I decided to take a deeper route into the medical world to compare the two. I enrolled in college to become a Certified Medical Assistant. The program lasted 9 months and I was hired in by one of the talent scouts that did the mock interviews at the end of the program. I made the deans list every semester with a GPA of 3.8 and an attendance rate of 92%. Juggling school with two jobs was challenging but it felt good to have an upgraded pay that afforded me the ability to quit the two jobs that I was not passionate about. Life was good, I had a good job, a nice apartment, a car and joy.

Two years went by before I realized that even as I showed up to that job everyday, something inside me kept whispering that I was meant for more. Not in a loud, rebellious way; more like a quiet tug, a reminder that the gifts I carried were asking for a bigger room to breathe. The more I grew in awareness, the more impossible it became to shrink myself into roles that no longer fit. It was as if the gifts inside me were begging me not to forget them.

Just a year later I became a mother. I was ecstatic! Becoming a mom had forced me to think about the future of my sons well-being. One decision, one aligned choice at a time and with each step, life continued to respond in ways I could've never predicted; kids, doors opening, opportunities finding me, and recognition arriving long before I thought I was "ready."

Moving forced me to face the truth that I was no longer the woman I had been in my previous chapters. After all, Staying where I was born and raised felt so comfortable that it started to become uncomfortable and posed a threat to my growth. I'd spent so long surviving, healing, releasing, and re-discovering myself that I hadn't realized I'd outgrown the spaces that once fit me. Accepting that wasn't easy. It required me to surrender the image of who I thought I needed to be and make room for who I really was. For the first time, I allowed myself to start fresh without apologizing for it. I gave myself permission to build a life that felt like home, not just a life that looked stable from the outside. That acceptance opened the door for everything that followed.

As my environment shifted, so did I. My family grew. My 2 children Nyaire and Naedene taught me more about unconditional love, surrender, and patience than any book or mentor ever could. Motherhood expanded me. It reminds me that abundance isn't something you chase, it's something you create through intention, love and courage. Thankfully, I'd also like to add a reminder that God has the last say because according to what a Dr. told me in chapter one, I wouldn't be able to have children...BUT GOD!

Every moment from juggling bottles and dreams, to late-night tears and early-morning determination taught me that abundance is not measured by ease, but by meaning, and my life was overflowing with meaning. With that same love, I poured myself into building businesses that would give my children a foundation later in their lives. I didn't start businesses with certainty, I started them with faith. Faith that my story mattered.

Faith that my gifts could serve others, and faith that purpose always provides. As I operated from alignment, doors opened, opportunities unfolded and unexpected blessings found their way to me.

Being recognized in magazines such as Canvas Rebel, Voyage OH, and Connected Woman mag (just to name a few) didn't feel like a finish line. It felt like confirmation that the seeds I had planted during my hardest seasons were finally rising toward the light. Those recognitions weren't proof of my worth. They were reflections of my growth.

Living in full bloom didn't mean becoming perfect, it meant becoming real. I no longer hid my scars to appear strong. I no longer softened my brilliance to make others comfortable. I no longer molded myself into who I thought I "should" be. Authenticity became my freedom. I learned that when you stop performing and start presenting your true self, life shifts. People hear you differently and opportunities see you differently and you see yourself differently too. My authenticity came from surrendering the roles, narratives, and expectations that kept me small.

Living in full bloom meant my thoughts, choices, relationships, dreams, habits, and spirit were finally moving in the same direction. I wasn't fragmented anymore. I wasn't fighting myself or chasing validation. I was rooted, balanced and whole. And for the first time in my life, I felt like I belonged to myself. This chapter isn't the end of my story, it's the beginning of a new season. Full bloom isn't something that life gives you, it's something that you chose everyday and with each choice, you blossom a little more.

I moved to a new state but the real journey was moving into myself. I built a family, but I also built a woman I am proud to be. I launched businesses, but I also launched a new chapter of purpose. I earned recognition, but I also earned inner peace. This is what it means to live in full bloom. To stand tall in your truth, rise from your roots, shine without asking permission and to harvest the life your soul always knew was possible.

Growth isn't about becoming someone new. It's about remembering who you were before the world told you who to be. By now, you've realized that your thoughts are powerful enough to plant or poison your future. You've faced the discomfort of reverting to old habits, and you've felt the reward of staying consistent long enough to see a harvest. ***Now comes the fourth and fifth levels of self-awareness; expression and integration***. When awareness becomes a lifestyle, you no longer "practice" self-awareness, you ARE self aware. You start to share your truth, creating, inspiring and expressing who you freely are. Your thoughts choices and actions naturally bear fruit that nourishes you and those around you. This is wholeness, not perfection, but peace.

Surrender & detachment

Blooming requires letting go. Not of your dreams, but of your fear of how they will happen. Surrender isn't giving up. It's releasing control so alignment can take the lead. When I stopped clinging and started trusting, life began to unfold in ways I could never have forced. Detachment gave me peace. Surrender gave me clarity. Trust gave me freedom.

Authenticity

Authenticity became one of the greatest gifts of my bloom. For years I shaped myself around survival. I adjusted my tone, softened my truths and fit into environments that didn't fit me back. But when I stepped into the fullness of who I was becoming, I realized that authenticity isn't an act, its a homecoming. When you stop performing, life stops performing too. It becomes real with you. It becomes aligned with you. Authenticity became the bridge between who I had been and who I was becoming. When I started walking across it, I realized the world had been waiting for the real me the entire time.

Integration

Integration is the quiet but powerful merging of your healed parts with your present self. It's where your inner work finally becomes instinct, not effort. If alignment is choosing to live your truth consistently, integration is becoming that truth naturally. This is the moment when the roots you cultivated grow deep enough to nourish you without constant tending. You inner soil is stabilized, rich and self-sustaining. The garden no longer needs rescuing, it is thriving from within. Internal signs of integration include, compassionate self-talk and catching misalignment before it grows. Emotional maturity becomes default, and peace feels familiar, not foreign. Integration is where healing becomes identity.

Expression

If integration is becoming whole, expression is sharing that wholeness with the world. Expression is the natural overflow of a cultivated inner world. It is you living soft, transparent and grounded. This is strength without performance and power without pretending. Expression creates impact because your healed life becomes a living example in a way that your fruit inspires others. Your boundaries teach others, your voice liberates others, your authenticity gives others permission and your transparency models freedom. Expression is the season where your healing becomes service. Your life becomes the garden that others learn from, rest in and grow beside.

Abundance- Living From Overflow

When your inner world is healthy, your other worlds reflect it. Abundance is not about how much you have; it's about how much you embody. People who live in full bloom don't chase- they cultivate. They understand that the more love, peace, and gratitude they nurture inside, the more they have to give away. You've done the inner work. You've faced the uncomfortable seasons. Now it's time to live from the overflow, to let what you've learned become how you live. Don't wait for everything to be perfect before you share your growth. Someone's breakthrough might depend on your transparency.

Action Step

Practice overflow. Do one thing each day that pours into someone else- a word of encouragement, a kind act, or even sharing your story. That's how you multiply your growth.

The Final Harvest

CHAPTER 4: LIVING IN FULL BLOOM

Self-awareness begins as a seed awakening in the darkness (realization). It deepens as roots search for understanding (reflection). It strengthens as the sprout rises with intention (alignment). It becomes whole as the bloom unfolds from within (integration). And it reaches it's fullness when it shares its beauty and fruit with the world (expression). This is the beautiful journey of becoming.

As you close this book, I hope you feel something awakening inside you. Not a rush to change your entire life at once, but a gentle reminder that transformation begins within. The Fruit of My Thoughts is not just the story of my becoming; it's an invitation for you to return to yourself, to water the places you've neglected, and to honor the seeds of truth already planted within you. You are worthy of your own awareness. You are deserving of your own healing, and you are capable of blooming in ways you haven't even imagined yet. Your life is a garden, and every thought is a seed. Choose the ones that lead you toward light. If these words have shown you anything, let it be this: You don't have to wait for permission, clarity, or perfection to begin. You only need the courage to grow. From here forward, may you nurture the kind of thoughts that blossom into a life you're proud to call your own.

Acknowledgments

To every soul who has ever felt stuck, overlooked, and uncertain this book is for you. I am deeply grateful to the mentors who lit the path ahead of me, the friends who challenged me to grow, and the quiet struggles that shaped these lessons. Your courage to turn the page and seek change inspires me more than you know.

To my children Nyaire and Naedene- thank you for showing me true unconditional love. I love you both more than you know. To my partner Jay Stallworth and my friend Chad Grant...thank you for believing in me without a doubt and listening to me as I expressed ideas and inspirations.

About the Author

Angel Inspires is a transformational speaker, certified life and health coach, and founder of a growing personal development brand dedicated to helping individuals reclaim their power. After navigating her own path through self-doubt, conditioning, and awakening, Angel rebuilt her life from the inside out transitioning from employee to entrepreneur and earning recognition in several magazines along the way.

Her work is rooted in transparency, alignment, and self-awareness. Angel uses her story as a blueprint for others, teaching that true transformation begins the moment you choose yourself. ***The Fruit of My Thoughts*** captures the insights, lessons, and breakthrough that shaped her evolution.

www.ingramcontent.com/pod-product-compliance
Lightning Source LLC
Chambersburg PA
CBHW020653060526
44119CB00069B/28